VA
ANI

By the same author:

The Case of Valentin Tomberg

The Cycle of the Seasons and the Seven Liberal Arts

The Cycle of the Year as a Path of Initiation

The East in the Light of the West

The Encounter with Evil and its Overcoming through Spiritual Science

Eternal Individuality, Towards a Karmic Biography of Novalis

The Heavenly Sophia and the Living Being Anthroposophia

May Human Beings Hear it!

The Mystery of John the Baptist and John the Evangelist

The Occult Significance of Forgiveness

Prophecy of the Russian Epic

Rudolf Steiner and the Founding of the New Mysteries

Rudolf Steiner's Research into Karma and the Mission of the Anthroposophical Society

The Spiritual Origins of Eastern Europe and the Future Mysteries of the Holy Grail

The Twelve Holy Nights and the Spiritual Hierarchies

VALENTIN TOMBERG AND ANTHROPOSOPHY

A Problematic Relationship

SERGEI O. PROKOFIEFF

TEMPLE LODGE

Translated from German by Peggy Elliott

Temple Lodge Publishing
Hillside House, The Square
Forest Row, RH18 5ES

www.templelodge.com

First English edition 2005

Originally published in German under the title *Die Beziehung des späteren Tomberg zu Rudolf Steiner zur Anthroposophie* by Verlag am Goethenum, Dornach, in 2003

A catalogue record for this book is available from the British Library

ISBN 1 902636 64 3

Cover by Andrew Morgan
Typeset by DP Photosetting, Aylesbury, Bucks.
Printed and bound by Cromwell Press Limited, Trowbridge, Wilts.

Contents

Prefatory Note

My book *Der Fall Tomberg, Anthroposophie oder Jesuitismus* was first published by Verlag am Goetheanum, Dornach, in 1995. A second, enlarged edition, co-authored by Christian Lazaridès, was self published in Germany in 1996.

The English edition, *The Case of Valentin Tomberg*, published by Temple Lodge in 1997, is based on the enlarged edition of 1996 but excludes the chapter written by Christian Lazaridès.

Seven years after the publication of the 1996 German edition, the book received renewed criticism in the magazine *Novalis*. I was given the opportunity to comment on this criticism (*Novalis*, Nos. 1/2, 3/4 and 5/6 2003). Working on my reply resulted in my writing the three essays constituting this present work. They deal further with problems relating to Tomberg and may be considered as additional chapters to the previous book.

Sergei Prokofieff
Dornach, May 2003

1. Three Testimonies from Tomberg's Own Hand

Recently the myth has circulated in anthroposophical circles that Valentin Tomberg's conversion from anthroposophy to Roman Catholicism in the 1940s was at the behest of Rudolf Steiner from the spiritual world. It is often added that during the second period of his life Tomberg continued to remain in spiritual contact with Rudolf Steiner, i.e. even at the time of working on his later, Catholic writings.[1]

This notion is refuted by facts documented by Tomberg himself. On 9 March 1970 Tomberg wrote a letter from Reading, England, the contents of which must at last be revealed. This is important because extracts of this letter that were published earlier don't give the reader a true idea of its contents.[2] In this letter, which was written only three years before his death, Tomberg, as far as is known today, comes to his final and most decisive conclusion about anthroposophy and Rudolf Steiner. And unless we find later, contradictory written evidence from Tomberg, this letter must be seen as a kind of testimony. Here follows the text of this letter, originally written in German, in the English translation:

Dr V. Tomberg
3 Newlands Avenue, Caversham, Reading, Berks.
9 March 1970.[3]

Dear Mr —

Here is a late—but well-considered—reply to your letter of 15.1.1970 which I have read and pondered thoroughly. My main question and worry is, how could I save you an expensive disappointment. Because a disappointment is unavoidable if you came to Reading to meet me personally; you would not encounter the one who emerged as the author of the 'Studies'[4] in the thirties and who represented a centrally focused spiritual science—simply for the reason that he isn't here any more, he no longer exists.

The author of the 'Studies' concerning the Bible and the Gospel was a man who had made it his task to save Rudolf Steiner's life work—spiritual science—from eradication and sclerosis by bringing it back to its central focus. However, the 'inner descendant' of this same person today believes that there is no 'spiritual science' and never can be. Because even a 'spiritual science' based on its central focus can only add momentum to the mill of death. It will unavoidably become intellectualized and 'fossilized'. Also spiritual science never existed because the essential criteria for every science must be that it can be tested, and that it applies universally. In reality, relating to the religious element, it was liberal theology or 'theology on its own initiative', and in an anthropological or psychological sense, a generalization of personal, psychological experiences. Whilst the experiences themselves are mystical they cannot claim a status that is scientific—universally applicable or verifiable.

It follows that so-called 'spiritual science' can only be psychologically convincing on the basis of a faithful endorsement by a particular group of people, objectively, however, only on the basis of trust in the account of the witness, i.e. authority. No pope has ever demanded of mankind such an extent of trust as the 'spiritual scientist' or initiate Rudolf Steiner. The pontiffs represent tradition, with hundreds of witnesses, whilst the 'spiritual scientist' draws on his own experiences and their interpretations and not out of tradition, and, whether intentional or not, demands an authority which rivals that of the Pope. Alas, like the Anti-Pope. None of this is spiritual science, which doesn't mean that there isn't and never was knowledge of the spirit. But knowledge of the spirit is not science but inner certainty—that means it is a condition that cannot be imposed on someone else. In any case it has to forgo any claim to universal validity and scrutiny. It is based on the most personal inner experience and can possibly only be shared with very close companions, close friends who have been joined through destiny.

This is the spiritual change that has happened to the Valentin Tomberg of the thirties: he no longer has a relationship to spiritual science, which he believes to be abstract.

Also the physical change since then has been enormous. He celebrated his 70th birthday nearly a week ago, and recently underwent a major operation from which he has barely recovered. He finds socializing and communication with people rather difficult. Today he can only bear the life of a recluse, e.g. he spent his 70th birthday with a party of seven visitors, the consequence of which was a painful sleepless night and a few days of depression!

You see, dear Mr — you will not encounter the Valentin Tomberg of the thirties. The distance which separates me from him today is as big as two incarnations. Really I should now have a different name; but for civil reasons that is not possible. Nothing lies further from me today or would be more tiring than to see the ashes of the anthroposophical past raised up.

Save yourself the shock of disappointment and shield me from discussions about the 'Studies', methods of work and similar things, which are now totally alien to me. Today my life is prayer and contemplation, and that—and only that—is what I live for; not 'study'.

In the sincere hope that you will understand.

Yours faithfully,
Valentin Tomberg

Reading this letter of the 70-year-old Tomberg one may be shocked at how bitterly and absolutely he refutes the existence of Rudolf Steiner's spiritual science. Equally negative is his condemnation of Rudolf Steiner. His Christology is labelled as 'theology on its own initiative' and Rudolf Steiner as the 'Anti-Pope' who as 'spiritual scientist' and 'initiate' demands his followers give him more authority than the 'infallible' Roman Pontiff himself.

This condemnation of Rudolf Steiner is even more surprising as it comes from the pen of one who at the beginning of the twenties twice personally approached Rudolf Steiner by letter asking to become his spiritual pupil and who later emerged with various publications as an anthroposophical author.

Even worse is his characterization of spiritual science itself. According to Tomberg it doesn't exist and even 'it never existed'; what existed was only Rudolf Steiner's 'generalizations of personal, deeply psychological experiences', i.e. a kind of 'mystic', with no claim to any scientific value—universal validity and standing up to scrutiny.

Paradoxically this judgement not only relates to Rudolf Steiner and anthroposophy but, above all, also to the early writings of Tomberg himself, which he based completely on the spiritual science of Rudolf Steiner and therefore described them as 'anthroposophical', i.e. 'spiritual studies'. Even if, at the beginning of his letter, Tomberg says that his 'Studies' of the thirties were 'spiritual science with a renewed central focus', now, at the end of his life, he is of the opinion that 'spiritual science cannot and does not exist' and that therefore also his own 'spiritual science with a renewed central focus [. . .] can only add momentum to the mill of death'. It is dead and 'pointless' for the 70-year-old Tomberg. He no longer has 'a relation to it' and expressly does not wish any connection with 'the ashes of his anthroposophical past'. This final reckoning with Rudolf Steiner, anthroposophy and his own early anthroposophical writings could not be more clearly and definitely documented.

*

Two further aspects of this letter merit our attention. The main argument that Tomberg produces against Rudolf Steiner, i.e. the spiritual science that he founded is only subjective 'mysticism', is taken up anew against Rudolf Steiner in two Jesuit publications some years later with almost the same wording: first in the book by Bernhard Grom, *Anthroposophie und Christentum* (Anthroposophy and Christianity), Munich 1989, and later in the publication by Fridolin Marxer and Andreas Traber, *Reinkarnation, Hoffnung oder Illusion* (Reincarnation, Hope or Illusion), Zürich 1995. In the latter, which is based on the former, it is stated that Rudolf Steiner's whole karma research developed purely out of 'inner feeling' and 'inner sensitivity' and: 'It can be argued that this path of knowledge, like mystical experience, cannot be communicated and above all it is not empirically verifiable' (p. 43). As it is almost certain that the two Jesuits didn't know of Tomberg's letter quoted above, one can only explain the similarity of their concepts concerning anthroposophy and its founder as coming through the same source of inspiration in the spiritual world.

The second aspect of this letter concerns Tomberg himself.

After his conversion he wants to regard himself as a completely different being who doesn't have and doesn't want to have anything further to do with the anthroposophical Tomberg of the thirties. And whilst the one Tomberg was full of enthusiasm for anthroposophy and convinced of its truthfulness, 'the inner descendant of this very same person' now believes that there is no 'spiritual science and there never can be'. The abyss which separates the 'anthroposophical' Tomberg from the later 'Catholic' one is of such depth for him as the abyss between two earthly lives: 'The distance which today separates me from him [he continually speaks of the earlier Tomberg in the third person] is as great as the one that separates two incarnations.'

Then follows an even more amazing confession: 'I actually should have a different name; but due to civil reasons that is not possible.' In other words, no trace, not even the name, should remain for posterity, only the later, 'Catholic' Tomberg and his works. This is because the early 'Tomberg' with his 'anthroposophical' writings 'exists no longer' but in his place is a totally different man.

Reading these words one can well understand that the old Tomberg didn't want a republication of his 'anthroposophical' early works or, according to another handed down version, that he would have preferred to see them as non-existent. Everything anthroposophical is now 'totally alien' to him.

One could not characterize in psychological or spiritual-scientific terms a personality split, which goes as far as a complete transformation, more precisely than is portrayed in this letter. Tomberg himself writes about a deep 'spiritual change that has happened to the Valentin Tomberg of the thirties'.

Without being aware of the contents of this letter at the

time of writing my part of the book about Tomberg, I myself came to the conclusion, through the discrepancy between his early and his later works, as well as the discrepancy between his late works and the writings of Rudolf Steiner, that this phenomenon could only be described in spiritual-scientific terms as a kind of 'occult imprisonment'.

There is a remarkable historical parallel handed down through Rudolf Steiner which demonstrates the basic possibility of such an occult phenomenon.

History relates that the personality who contributed most to the destruction of the highly spiritual Irish-Scottish Christianity on the Continent was himself a former Irish monk who later converted to Roman Catholicism: Winifrid-Boniface (*c.* 680–755). The reason for his success in destroying Irish-Scottish Christianity was that he knew it so well from the inside rather than only from the outside. As an explanation for this transformation of the Irish monk Winifrid to the enemy of Irish Christianity Boniface, Rudolf Steiner told Alexander Strakosch the following. On his journey from Britain to Rome Winifrid came to the Lerin Islands (off the southern coast of France, near Cannes) where he found a monastery loyal to Rome. There Winifrid (the later Bonifazius) was put into 'occult imprisonment' in order that all his thinking and willing would now be in the service of Rome.[5]

*

So that the reader doesn't get the impression that the later Tomberg spoke against Rudolf Steiner and anthroposophy only in his private letters, there now follow two excerpts from his two most significant Catholic writings (one could give more examples, but that would go beyond the framework of this essay).

In his *Meditations on the Tarot* one finds the following declaration (on p. 390): 'Esoteric Christianity is entirely *within* exoteric Christianity; it does not exist—and cannot exist—separately from it' (italics Tomberg).

Yet, anthroposophy as the principal stream of esoteric Christianity of the twentieth century was founded by Rudolf Steiner outside exoteric Christianity, which for Tomberg is identical with the Roman Catholic Church, and it continues to exist outside it to this day (see above). That means, however, that anthroposophy, as a stream of esoteric Christianity outside the Church, principally 'does not exist—and cannot exist' for the later Tomberg. This says more or less the same as Tomberg later wrote in his quoted letter only that by naming Rudolf Steiner and anthroposophy it has become more defined.

One just has to imagine what such an utterance means in spiritual-historical terms. It is exactly because of this kind of view that for example the whole of the Cathar stream of southern France was wiped out lock, stock and barrel by Rome at the beginning of the thirteenth century. A certain kind of esoteric Christianity then lived within the Cathar stream which according to Rome could not be allowed to exist outside the Church, therefore the Cathars were asked to voluntarily convert to Roman Catholicism or be destroyed. As they refused the former, the latter happened, above all through the leader of the crusade against the Cathars, Simon de Montfort, who devastated the land of the Cathars and their highly spiritual culture and wonderful social structures in 1212.[6]

*

Tomberg writes about the scientific character of anthroposophy in his second Catholic work, *Lazarus komm heraus*

(Lazarus Come Forth),[7] wholly in the sense of his letter as follows:

> Also it happened, however, for reasons which we need not go into here, that Rudolf Steiner gave his work the form of a science, so-called 'spiritual science'. Thereby the third aspect of the indivisible threefoldness of the Way, the Truth, and the Life—namely Life—was not given enough attention. For the scientific form into which the logic of the Logos had to be cast, and by which it was limited, left little room for pure mysticism and spiritual magic, that is, for Life [p. 70, English edition].

Here nothing less than that Rudolf Steiner forced the 'logic of the Logos' into the 'scientific form' of anthroposophy is proclaimed and that due to this anthroposophy came into the world without 'Life'.

In contrast, the reason why Rudolf Steiner gave anthroposophy a *scientific* character is that through it the central task of our time, the necessary connection between intellectuality and spirituality, can be resolved. Since the beginning of the epoch of the consciousness soul in the fifteenth century, the intellect is to be found increasingly in modern science. Anthroposophy raises it to a spiritual level and transforms it into a *science of the spirit*. In his lecture of 13 January 1924 (GA 233a*), Rudolf Steiner describes how this is achieved and how this task can only be fulfilled through a conscious encounter with Michael in the spiritual world.

In the words quoted from Tomberg and in particular in

---

* As all quotations from Rudolf Steiner have been translated afresh by the translator, references in the text are to German editions ('GA' standing for 'Gesamtausgabe', or 'Collected Works'). A list of relevant GAs appear on p. 54 with full titles and information about English published translations where relevant.

his letter it is noticeable how he only denies Rudolf Steiner the possibility of connecting intellectuality with spirituality, but not however Ignatius Loyola, the founder of the order of Jesuits, to whom he allocates this task in his *Meditations on the Tarot*.

The strongest remark by Tomberg against Rudolf Steiner is to be found in a further chapter of the same book: 'So there is in Anthroposophy a magnificent achievement of thought and will—which is, however, unmystical and unmagical, i.e. in want of Life. Rudolf Steiner himself was conscious of this essential lack.' (Page 70.)

This attack on Rudolf Steiner and his life's work is particularly grave as it implies a deliberate lie or intentional deception by Rudolf Steiner. According to Tomberg, Rudolf Steiner, despite being 'conscious of this essential lack', presented anthroposophy to the world as something full of life. The study of anthroposophy, however, reveals that anthroposophy itself is life as Rudolf Steiner expressed with the words: 'For life is the essential feature of its being. It is life flowing forth, from the spirit.' (GA 260a, 2, Letter to Members.)

Looking back at the life of Tomberg, it is particularly noteworthy that Marie Steiner, who was in regular contact with Tomberg in the thirties, already at that time sensed something of this attitude. Therefore she mentioned in her letter to Frau Dumpff (1936) that Tomberg denied Rudolf Steiner's insights a 'living force'.[8] She rightly calls this attitude of Tomberg occult conceit and personal arrogance.

Particularly striking is the fact that only a few years later Tomberg accuses Rudolf Steiner in the quoted letter of exactly the opposite, namely, that his anthroposophy is no spiritual science but mere subjective 'mysticism'.

This begs the question: if Tomberg in his book totally sets

out to refute that anthroposophy holds 'life', where does he himself find 'life' within Christianity? According to him, only where, as he believes, esoteric Christianity 'blossoms': *within* the Church. In later years he finds this above all in the Order of Jesuits and its 400-year history. Thus he writes in his *Meditations on the Tarot*: 'It is in this way that the living traditions represented by the Benedictine, Dominican, Franciscan, *Jesuit*, and also other orders, were founded. [. . .] *Thus* [. . .] *flourishes* [. . .] *the Jesuit order after four centuries*.' (P. 296, italics S.P.)

Tomberg admires the whole history of the Order of Jesuits up to our time without finding any flaw in it at all.[9] Above all he sees the importance of these 400 years of history largely in the fact that exactly this order, in so far as it uses the spiritual exercises of Ignatius Loyola as an occult basis, fulfils the task that Rudolf Steiner designated specifically as the core Michaelic task of anthroposophy, i.e. the above-mentioned union of intellectuality and spirituality.[10] The fact that Tomberg attributes this primary task of anthroposophy to the Order of Jesuits, knowing full well from his earlier work with anthroposophy what Rudolf Steiner said about this order and the spiritual exercises of Ignatius Loyola,[11] amounts to a further, heavy attack on anthroposophy.

*

Finally one may ask whether, based on these clear and unmistakable statements by Tomberg, one might find any truth at all in the myth we began with. Do today's followers of Tomberg really imagine that Rudolf Steiner would allow his work to be destroyed by Tomberg or let his person be so defamed? If it should indeed be true that, as Tomberg believed, his later writings were approved or even inspired by Rudolf Steiner, then it seems on the basis of the Tomberg statements quoted that this belonged to the greatest illusions of his life.

Only counter-forces that work from the spiritual world and that wish to destroy anthroposophy on earth can have inspired such statements, as were already present during the lifetime of Rudolf Steiner and are still present today in the attacks of the Jesuits against anthroposophy. According to the spiritual science of Rudolf Steiner, the Jesuits follow 'a different being [in the spiritual world] from the one that anthroposophy now has to follow for the good of mankind' (GA 197, 30 July 1920). Rudolf Steiner describes in various places that this 'other being' is able to reveal itself in manifold guises in the spiritual world, even in that of the Christ. That means that it could also appear as 'Rudolf Steiner' to Tomberg in order to destroy his work even more successfully, as the words of Tomberg show.

In the light of such massive attacks on Rudolf Steiner and anthroposophy by Tomberg one shouldn't be surprised that there have been and always will be anthroposophists who wish to defend the work and person of their teacher. This forms an essential part of the duties of a spiritual pupil. The book written by Christian Lazaridès and me also arose out of this feeling of duty. That is why it is not pro-active but a reaction to the defamation of anthroposophy and its founder.

2. The Anti-Rosicrucian Impulses in Tomberg's Later Works

Part of the strategy of the counter-forces is to ensure that human failure to recognize an illusion will produce further illusions.[12] One of these illusions, which appeared three years ago, will here be portrayed.

In an article to mark the 100th anniversary of Valentin Tomberg's birth, Michael Frensch mentions the occult law concerning the spiritual-historical rule of the Rosicrucian impulse as described by Rudolf Steiner and applies it directly to Tomberg's later works. By this law the Rosicrucian impulse reappears in a rhythm of 100 years. In his lecture of 27 September 1911 (GA 130) Rudolf Steiner gives as an example for the eighteenth century the appearance of the work *The Secret Symbols of the Rosicrucians* and for the nineteenth century *Isis Unveiled* by H.P. Blavatsky which arose out of this source (the latter, however, only in parts). Now Frensch poses the question: Where does one find the Rosicrucian impulse of the twentieth century? And he comes to the conclusion: 'I believe that there is only one single work that satisfies the demands of being a comprehensive summary of *Christian–Rosicrucian* wisdom in the twentieth century: *Meditations on the Tarot* by Tomberg.' (*Novalis* 4/2000, p. 22, italics M.F.)

It is immediately apparent that Rudolf Steiner, who represented the central Christian-Rosicrucian impulse of the twentieth century and who revealed the most important Rosicrucian mysteries, particularly in relation to Christian Rosenkreutz, himself finds no mention here. Frensch justifies this conclusion by pointing out that Rudolf Steiner spoke of a law of a hundred years that in the twentieth century, as in the eighteenth and nineteenth centuries, only comes to effect *at the end* of the century.

Frensch tries to substantiate this thesis by quoting Rudolf Steiner, but omits the decisive sentence without indicating this through the usual symbol of [...]. Therefore Rudolf Steiner's words are to be quoted here in full (the omitted sentence is in my italics): 'There is a law that this spiritual stream of force [that of Christian Rosenkreutz] has to become especially powerful approximately every hundred years. *This is now to be seen in the theosophical movement.* Christian Rosenkreutz gave an indication of this in his last exoteric statements' (p. 58).

Of course Rudolf Steiner doesn't use the word 'now' in relation to Annie Besant's oriental direction of the theosophical movement, he solely refers to the anthroposophical movement.[13]

From this quote it follows first of all that we are not dealing with exactly one hundred years but 'approximately a hundred years' and secondly that this law obviously operated differently in the twentieth century. The word 'now' in the omitted sentence makes this clear. The possible reasons for this may be that Blavatsky's Rosicrucian impulse very soon diverted into an eastern direction and Rudolf Steiner, in close cooperation with Christian Rosenkreutz, had to intervene correctively.

From everything that Rudolf Steiner said about Rosicrucianism and its founder it follows clearly and unmistakably that *he* is the main representative of Rosicrucianism in the twentieth century: 'Everything that is given as theosophy [anthroposophy] is being strengthened through the ether body of Christian Rosenkreutz, and those who bring theosophy [anthroposophy] are overshadowed by this ether body of Christian Rosenkreutz' (GA 130, 27 September 1911). This particularly includes Rudolf Steiner. In the same lecture he says further: 'Today Christian Rosenkreutz is incarnated,' i.e. in 1911. And one year later he says about himself that he is 'permitted to stand close to Christian Rosenkreutz' (GA 130, 18 December 1912).

If one therefore truly searches for the book representing the most comprehensive summary of modern Christian-Rosicrucian wisdom of the twentieth century then it must be Rudolf Steiner's *Occult Science*. Already prior to the publication of this book its contents were collated in the lecture cycle *Theosophy of the Rosicrucian** (1907, GA 99), which openly proclaimed his teachings as truly Rosicrucian. Also the sevenfold schooling path central to this book had been described by Rudolf Steiner as the Christian-Rosicrucian path in many previous lectures.[14]

In contrast, the reader will not discover anything of importance about Rosicrucianism or its founder in *Meditations on the Tarot*. This stream is forever brought into connection with a number of French occultists who founded a pseudo-Rosicrucian stream at the end of the nineteenth century and who worked with methods not permitted in true occultism.

The well-known Satanist S. Guaita, for example, who regarded himself as a 'Rosicrucian of the left hand', founded and led, together with Papus and J. Péladan, the 'Ordre Kabalistique de la Rose-Croix' in 1888.[15] Rudolf Steiner says of the second founder, Papus, that his occult methods are close to black magic.[16] And of J. Péladan it is known that he later converted to Roman Catholicism and founded his own order with the name 'Ordre de la Rose-Croix Cath-

* Published as *Rosicrucian Wisdom*, London 2000.

olique'.[17] All of these dubious occultists tried at that time to distort true Rosicrucianism in different ways and to use its name to bring an anti-Rosicrucian movement into the world.

In his *Meditations on the Tarot* Tomberg repeatedly names just these same occultists as those in the spiritual world from whom he received the most important inspirations. He writes: '... and how many times, in writing these Letters, have I felt the fraternal embraces of these Friends [in the spiritual world], including here Papus, Quaita, Péladan, Eliphas Lévi ...' (p. 391).[18]

In *Meditations on the Tarot* hardly anything is found about Rosicrucianism, except for a long quote by an H. Jennings against it (pp. 156–7). And nowhere in his book does Tomberg refer to as a source of inspiration either Christian Rosenkreutz, whose name isn't even mentioned, or Rudolf Steiner, who is only mentioned in passing alongside many other names whilst repeatedly referring to the abovementioned French occultists.

Therefore it doesn't come as a surprise that Tomberg, inspired by these pseudo-Rosicrucians, consistently pushes the true Rosicrucianism of the twentieth century, as revealed by anthroposophy, back to its medieval and therefore no longer appropriate forms. Thus in *Meditations on the Tarot* the central sign of Rosicrucianism in the twentieth century, the cross surrounded by *seven* roses, is replaced by the cross with only *one* rose in the middle in order to then bring it into total dependence on the cross *without* any roses.[19] Also, Tomberg replaces the second sentence of the Rosicrucian words which Rudolf Steiner gives as 'In Christo morimur' with 'In *Jesu* morimur' (*Covenant* ..., p. 79, italics S.P.). Yet in his central Christological cycle, Rudolf Steiner points to the path from Jesus to Christ as the basis of all anthroposophy. Tomberg surreptitiously, through this change of name, changes this back to 'Jesus' whom especially the Jesuits have put into the centre of their occult practices.[20]

But the situation becomes even more serious when Tomberg continues to write in *Meditations on the Tarot*: 'Therefore someone would certainly be in error if, instead of seeing in the Crucifix *the* way, *the* truth and *the* life, he were to think of founding, for example, a community or "fraternity of the Resurrection" with the Gilded Cross and rose of silver as its symbol, replacing the universal symbol of Christianity—the Crucifix.' According to his interpretation the rose cross cannot 'replace the Crucifix but are included and implied in it' (p. 390, italics Tomberg). These words carry a special meaning because shortly afterwards there follows the sentence quoted in Chapter 1 of this work which states that esoteric Christianity does not and cannot exist outside exoteric Christianity, and already on the next page he writes about inspirations through 'Papus, Guaita, Péladan' (p. 391).

It follows that according to Tomberg the Rosicrucian stream as the central stream of esoteric Christianity—whose esotericism is not based on the principle of death but on that of *resurrection*[21] and which can therefore rightly be called the 'Brotherhood of Resurrection' (and for this reason carries as its symbol the *cross with seven roses*)—cannot exist outside exoteric Christianity, i.e. the Church. This means that the founding and the spiritual work over centuries of the true Rosicrucians, which in particular served to pave the way for the reappearance of the Christ in the etheric,[22] is denied. It is difficult to imagine a stronger attack on the innermost core of true Rosicrucianism.

The occult background to this whole situation can be found in the works of Rudolf Steiner. The brotherhood of the

Rosicrucians came into being because it took the decisive step from the cross to the rose cross, i.e. from death to resurrection—or in other words, from Jesus to Christ–Jesus. In contrast the symbol of the *cross without roses* is that of the Order of Jesuits, which stands in polar opposition to Rosicrucianism. Therefore Rudolf Steiner says about the basic polarity of these two orders: '[One] stands for the cross on its own, without the roses. Another order, however, added the roses to the cross from which new life springs forth. We thus have two modern streams: one which has brought the old into the present and is intent on preventing progress with all its might; the other which has surrounded the old cross with roses and has implanted a fresh shoot, encircling the cross with roses. These two streams lived side by side: the order with the cross without roses; the other revering the roses on the cross—something new that is to come. The latter are the Rosicrucians. The theosophical movement is built on this stream [i.e. that part of the movement led by Rudolf Steiner]' (GA 93, 23 October 1905). It is of great importance that Rudolf Steiner always talks of *several* roses, because the picture of the cross with seven roses is today the symbol of the reappearance in the etheric.

Viewed from a spiritual-historical standpoint, the relationship between the Roman Catholic Church and true Rosicrucianism is marked by persecutions to the extent of near total outer extinction of this stream—persecutions based on the principle that esoteric Christianity cannot exist outside exoteric Christianity. For this reason nearly all esoteric streams were destroyed by the Church throughout the history of Christianity. Through centuries this contradiction existed and 'finds its expression in the fight of the Roman Catholic Church against the Templars, Rosicrucians, Albigensians, Cathars, etc. They are all wiped off the outer physical plane, but their inner life continues' (GA 93, 11 November 1904); and, I believe, today especially in anthroposophy.

The Catholic Tomberg, however, remains firm. Just as he denies the existence of spiritual science as such in his letter (see Chapter 1), he also denies the existence of true Rosicrucianism in his later work. Neither, according to his later understanding, can possibly exist outside the Church. He only makes a mention of them at all because of his connection with these streams during his 'anthroposophical' period. The destruction of the Order of Templars in contrast is not mentioned at all, and as regards the gruesome obliteration of the Cathars and Albigensians only a few fleeting words can be found in his later works, stating that they had all become 'victims of heresy'.

The persecution of the Rosicrucians by the Roman Catholic Church already existed at the time of the initiation of Christian Rosenkreutz in the thirteenth century. Rudolf Steiner describes the twelve wise men who initiated the thirteenth as follows: 'Now the twelve, being deeply devoted to their spiritual tasks and inwardly permeated with Christianity, were conscious that the external Christianity of the Church was only a caricature of the real Christianity. They were permeated with the greatness of Christianity, although outwardly they were taken to be its enemies' (GA 130, 27 September 1911). The latter means that already at that time they belonged to those persecuted by the Church.

This persecution intensified with the founding of the Order of Jesuits. *On the cover page* of his work *Fama Fraternitatis*, which arose out of Rosicrucian inspirations and which was written for the 'rulers, ranks and scholars of Europe' and in which the discovery of Christian Rosenkreutz's grave is described, Valentin Andreae (seventeenth century) therefore writes the following words: 'A short reply by Mr Haselmeyer

... who was imprisoned by the Jesuits for it and tied to the scaffold.'[23] And in the second Rosicrucian work *Confessio Fraternitatis*, concerning the 'Declaration'[24] of the Rosicrucian brotherhood and which equally addresses all 'scholars of Europe', one can find such a devastating critique of the Pope that can only be compared to Tomberg's own early utterances and that stands in total contradiction to his later works.[25]

To this also belongs the well-known persecution and manifold defamation of H.P. Blavatsky by the Jesuits due to the Rosicrucian sources of her early writings. And Rudolf Steiner mentions frequently that after he had exposed the anti-Christian character of the occult practices by Jesuits in his cycle *From Jesus to Christ* he also fell under this persistent persecution and defamation until the end of his life.[26] The fight of the Jesuits against anthroposophy, as the modern form of Rosicrucianism, continues to this day.[27]

The secret Rosicrucian Master of the young Rudolf Steiner, who was according to his words 'again as far as possible opposed to anything clerical', used 'particularly one book [...] that due to its anti-clerical tendency was often suppressed in Austria'.[28]

Thus we here have evidence (and there's much more) of the incompatibility of true Rosicrucianism with the Roman Catholic Church, particularly however for Rosicrucianism being the absolute opposite to the Jesuits and their occult practices. Therefore Tomberg denounced the methods of the Jesuits as 'satanic', when he held a Rosicrucian point of view during his occupation with anthroposophy.[29]

But how does Tomberg deal with this in his later book *Covenant of the Heart*? Well aware, through his earlier anthroposophical studies, that the founding of the Rosicrucian stream spiritually relates to the raising of Lazarus (see GA 265) and of the fact that the Rosicrucian initiation, as one connected to the spirit, is directly linked to the Whitsun event (see GA 131, 5 October 1911), he assigns these two main roots of Rosicrucianism to the Order of Jesuits. He seriously believes that the founding of the latter has its origins in the raising of Lazarus and the Whitsun event.[30]

As we have seen in Chapter 1, *Meditations on the Tarot* attributes the main task of anthroposophy (which is also the most important *Rosicrucian* mission of the present time, namely, to connect the intellectual and spiritual life) to Ignatius Loyola and his spiritual exercises, which to this day form the occult basis for the Order of Jesuits. Thus it denies Rudolf Steiner's statement that, 'In the development of civilization during the last few centuries there is hardly a greater contrast than that between Jesuitism and Rosicrucianism' (GA 131, 5 October 1911). The reason for this is that in the centre of Rosicrucian initiation, as maintained by anthroposophy today, *human freedom* stands as its central focus and highest ideal. By contrast Loyola regards as the highest ideal for his order that each member lets himself be 'guided and led ... like a corpse with neither will nor consciousness'.[31] The 'spiritual exercises' developed by him serve this purpose.[32]

In contrast, the most important task of the founder of the Order of Rosicrucians is to guide mankind towards finding the moral law within itself, i.e. to prepare them for what is today given to everyone in *The Philosophy of Freedom*. Rudolf Steiner says about this task that Christian Rosenkreutz and his seven pupils laid the foundation for the recognition of the moral law within each human being who would bring it to individual life, thus making it unnecessary to cling to external religion (GA 264, 10 November 1905).

The inner attitude, however, that stands in total opposition to the above is the one achieved by the Jesuit student through these 'exercises'. Ignatius Loyola's words, which Hans Urs von Balthasar[33] (an ex-Jesuit and perhaps strongest defender of these 'exercises' in the twentieth century) added to his translation because of their importance, confirm this: 'In order to achieve correctness in everything we always have to hold onto the following: I believe that the white I see is black, if the hierarchical Church defines it such.' These words are a real slap in the face of the consciousness soul! But they show how the Order of Jesuits with its 'exercises' was founded in order to fight the rise of the consciousness soul within humanity. Particularly in the Order of Jesuits, through their 'exercises', every bit of individual freedom and autonomy of the human I is opposed by the hierarchical order of the Church, resulting in absolute and unconditional obedience.

Tomberg shares this conviction with the Jesuits. In *Meditations on the Tarot* he writes: 'The impulse of freedom—of hope in emancipated man—has [. . .] created a materialistic civilisation without parallel, but at the same time it has destroyed the hierarchical order—the order of spiritual obedience. A series of religious, political and social revolutions has ensued.

'But the hierarchical order is eternal and obedience is indispensable' (p. 119).[34]

Therefore the greatest contradiction in the epoch of the consciousness soul remains the contradiction between Rudolf Steiner's *ethical individualism* based on human freedom and Ignatius Loyola's 'cadaver obedience'. And in the fight for humanity's individual freedom, no doubt this is where each one will have to go their own different way today and in the future.

There are still people alive today who personally heard Tomberg say, during his Catholic period, that he regarded the development of the consciousness soul as having failed. Therefore in his later works he looked for a way that was to lead directly from the sentient soul to the Spirit Self.[35] This meant, however, that the whole development of the free autonomous individuality of the human being as well as the possibility of a direct and conscious relationship to the spiritual world (without the intercession of the Church), is fundamentally denied. As a consequence of this attitude of bypassing the consciousness soul, however, the Spirit Self can only be reached in a *luciferic* manner because the past is carried directly into the future without consideration of the forces of the present through which Christ works today in his etheric form.

This inner attitude explains Tomberg's conversion to Catholicism and his subsequent fight against anthroposophy (see Chapter 1), because without the consciousness soul anthroposophy cannot develop. Therefore every human being following the Christian path yet denying the development of the consciousness soul whilst looking for spirituality, necessarily has to fall back into the lap of the Roman Catholic Church, fully supporting its old, conservative tendencies and inclinations. That is what happened to Tomberg. With all his immense occult knowledge, for example, he defended the recognition and spiritual 'reasoning' of the infallibility of the Pope as it was proclaimed at the first Vatican council in 1869/70.[36] This very dogma was established in order to prevent the development of the consciousness soul in the western world.

It is therefore noteworthy that Tomberg rejected the weak and failed attempt of the Roman Catholic Church (failed because the infallibility dogma was its downfall) to minimally adapt to the demands of the epoch of the consciousness soul at the second Vatican Council. The ex-Catholic priest and Tomberg-follower Wilhelm Maas writes in this connection: 'Tomberg was unable to sympathize with the view of the second Vatican Council. He was generally opposed to its decisions.'[37]

At the end of his essay (see above) Frensch refers to the anonymity of *Meditations on the Tarot*, which he had newly translated into German and which Tomberg wrote under the pseudonym 'Anonymus d'ourtre tombe' and with the address 'a friend from beyond the grave', as most important evidence of Tomberg's connection to Christian Rosenkreutz. But herein lies a fundamental paradox, in that *Meditations on the Tarot* had already been translated into German earlier—whilst Tomberg was still alive—and, known to him, was first published in Germany anonymously (1972), so that the readers of this book were deliberately led to believe that the author was dead and acted 'from beyond the grave'.[38] Tomberg justifies this anonymity in his book as follows: 'I am an anonymous author and I remain so in order to be able to be more frank and sincere than is ordinarily permitted to an author' (p. 61)—truly a strange remark in the epoch of the consciousness soul! As if Rudolf Steiner or at the time the Apostles and Evangelists who always wrote under their own name had *therefore* been less 'frank' and 'sincere'.

From an anthroposophical point of view, however, concerning any kind of anonymity in our time, Rudolf Steiner says the following: 'If the author does not take responsibility for his writing, the principle of the theosophical movement is broken. If it was to be claimed anywhere that a book was written without the responsibility of the author you know that this cannot be true but that it is a luciferic-ahrimanic deception. Today's Masters do not permit an author to deny responsibility' (GA 130, 17 June 1912).[39] Christian Rosenkreutz in particular, of whom Rudolf Steiner speaks before and after the quoted words, doesn't permit this today. Therefore nobody who follows Christian

Rosenkreutz in the epoch of the consciousness soul can bring anything into the world anonymously. There has to be an actual human 'I' that stands behind it and bears witness with its earthly name.

Rudolf Steiner also emphasizes again and again that on the basis of true Rosicrucianism neither any principle of authority nor any compelling dogma can be warranted (see for example GA 121, 17 June 1910). It follows that today anthroposophy, as the representative of true Rosicrucianism in the epoch of the consciousness soul, stands opposed to the dogma of infallibility of the first Vatican Council and consequently its increasingly dogmatic Church. In contrast the later Tomberg justified and supported it unconditionally.[40]

The decisive fact, however, is that in Tomberg's later works the etheric Christ finds no mention at all and this shows clearly that there can be no indication of a relationship with Christian Rosenkreutz or his etheric body as Frensch claims despite all evidence.

Rudolf Steiner in contrast, from the year 1910 onwards[41] until his death, proclaimed this central event of the twentieth century untiringly and added new aspects to it again and again (the last in September 1924).

Therefore there is no logical reason to connect Tomberg's anti-Rosicrucian *Meditations on the Tarot* in any form at all to the noble founder of Rosicrucianism who stands together with Rudolf Steiner at the altar of Christ.[42]

3. Platonists and Aristotelians as seen by some Tombergians

Three years after the turn of the century and as time goes by one can become increasingly concerned about the question as to what happened to Rudolf Steiner's prophecy regarding the turn of the century. What happened to the realization of the *irrevocable* contract made in the spiritual world between Platonists and Aristotelians to work together on earth at the end of the twentieth century in the service of anthroposophy?

In any case it seems evident that anthroposophy has neither made a cultural breakthrough within humanity nor developed into a culturally creative force as Rudolf Steiner expected in connection with its possible culmination at the end of the century. Therefore, what has been said could also be formulated in the following way: Has this culmination not happened at all or has it perhaps not happened *yet*? Has the working together of Platonists and Aristotelians already become a reality on earth, or not yet? Today every anthroposophist has to live with this disturbing and not easy to answer question.

In this chapter I do not intend to pursue this question further because I have already expressed my point of view in the second part of my essay 'The End of the Century and the Tasks of the Anthroposophical Society'.[43] In it I pointed out that Rudolf Steiner envisaged the culmination of anthroposophy at the end of the century and thus the possibility of a coming together of Platonists and Aristotelians on earth dependent on definite and clearly outlined *conditions*, under which alone this 'Michael-prophecy' can be fulfilled.

The most important of these conditions is the deepening

understanding and right nurturing of the spiritual impulse of the Christmas Conference within the Anthroposophical Society. For only this Christmas Conference enabled Rudolf Steiner to present to the members their Michaelic karma as well as to speak about the prophecy connected with it concerning the end of the century.[44]

If one looks at the history of the Anthroposophical Society from this angle it becomes apparent that although the impulse of the Christmas Conference has been carried in full consciousness and carefully nurtured by some individual members, with time it nevertheless began to disappear from the wider circles of the Society so that today one has to begin again to work with and enliven this impulse.

So we face the distressing reality that the main condition on which the culmination at the turn of the century depends has not been fulfilled, or at least not sufficiently, within the Anthroposophical Society. We can see the consequences of this in our present situation (including the debates about the constitution which are the resulting unfortunate substitute for our lack of spiritual endeavour in this area).

This tragic situation, however, should not lead us to becoming resigned to it but instead to contemplate that time is of the essence when fulfilling the conditions for the emergence on earth of the two groups. In the epoch of freedom, in which we live, much more depends on mankind's free decision-making than is widely imagined. Therefore, I believe, one cannot constantly speak of a lack of fulfilment of the prophecy (as some anthroposophists do), but rather speak of a certain delay as regards these conditions. In other words: only through the fulfilment of these conditions can the mutually agreed tasks between Platonists and Aristotelians begin on earth. When this will happen and whether it will be able to bring about the culmination of the anthroposophical movement under the then existing human conditions, which will be very different in the next decades from those at the turn of the century, remains a question which cannot possibly be answered theoretically. But what can be said with certainty is that—come what may—the Platonists and Aristotelians will honour their heavenly agreement on earth, which Rudolf Steiner calls 'irrevocable', even if it is delayed and comes in a different form.

In order to understand the future cooperation of the two groups better and to begin with its practical preparations, one first of all has to look at the two-stage heavenly preparation of anthroposophy in which both groups played an equally central role. Rudolf Steiner describes the first stage as the all-encompassing School of Michael in the Sun-sphere. In it Michael emerged as the leading Sun archangel who, according to Rudolf Steiner's comparison, stands as much above all other archangels as the sun stands above all the planets.[45] This unique position of Michael within the circle of archangels leading mankind is particularly significant in that he appears as the countenance of Christ, i.e. as that archangel who amongst all others predominantly represents the forces of the Christ as the highest Sun Being in their environment. This closeness to the Christ Being also means that Michael is much more connected to the final goal of human development than the other archangels. This goal is the creation of a new hierarchy in the cosmos, the hierarchy of freedom and love. Because true love as the highest creative force of the universe is unobtainable without freedom, Michael appears to mankind as its cosmic ideal or, as Rudolf Steiner calls him, as the 'spiritual hero of freedom'.[46]

This cosmic position of Michael, which wholly accepts human freedom and which above all is founded on his special relationship to the Christ Being, is not fully shared by the other six archangels, least of all by the archangel of Saturn—Oriphiel.[47] Therefore Michael's position within the circle of archangels and hence his connection to human evolution is particularly dramatic. This drama has been intensifying since humanity entered into the epoch of freedom, i.e. since the beginning of the fifth post-Atlantian epoch or the epoch of the consciousness soul.

Yet even through this crisis Michael remains true to the impulse of freedom. Particularly because he knows that the possibility of freedom was given to mankind through the Christ deed on Golgotha, i.e. through that Being whom he has served as Sun archangel since the beginning. Rudolf Steiner points to this in the following way: 'Through this alone [the Mystery of Golgotha] the freedom of man, the complete dignity of man, first became possible. For us to be free beings, we owe gratitude to a divine act of love. As humans we can feel ourselves as free beings, but must never forget that we owe this freedom to the divine deed of love of the Gods [. . .]. Men should not be able to attain the concept of freedom without the concept of redemption through Christ. Only then is the thought of freedom justified' (GA 131, 14 October 1911). These words, the result of Rudolf Steiner's spiritual research, show at the same time the highest recognition for Michael and his unyielding strength in the spiritual world to stand up for human freedom. Because for him this means that he must put himself into the service of the Mystery of Golgotha and be a servant of Christ even after Christ has left the Sun-sphere.

From a human point of view it now becomes clear why Rudolf Steiner's book *The Philosophy of Freedom* can be called the most Christian book of our time. In it is described the path to freedom, which at the same time is the path to experience the Mystery of Golgotha. In Rudolf Steiner's autobiography we can find how he, following this path unfailingly, came to the spiritual experience of the Mystery of Golgotha (GA 28, Chapter 26).[48]

In the 'Michael Letters' (*Anthroposophical Leading Thoughts*), which Rudolf Steiner wrote towards the end of his life (GA 26), he describes in detail how the being of human freedom is rooted in the cosmic Michael Mystery. Michael, as Sun-servant of the Christ, today wants to open up the path to humanity which leads from *The Philosophy of Freedom* to Christ-knowledge and on to Christ-experience. Therefore Rudolf Steiner speaks in the Michael Letters of the 'Michael-Christ experience of man'. For in our time a fully conscious relationship to the Christ is only possible through the Michaelic path. In order to prepare this path the great supersensible School was founded by Michael himself between the fifteenth and seventeenth centuries in the Sun-sphere. And when Rudolf Steiner says that a 'new Christianity' was prepared in this School of Michael then this is the Christianity of freedom which was founded through anthroposophy on earth in the twentieth century.

Both streams, Aristotelians and Platonists alike, participated *equally* in the preparation of this future Christianity in the School of Michael and since then carry within themselves the impulse of the new Michaelic Christianity in the highest sense. Today, therefore, these two streams no longer have anything in common with the traditionally handed down or institutionalized forms of Christianity in the way they have been preserved on earth, particularly by the leading Churches. The Churches represent the kind of Christianity which stems from the old earthly traditions and which has *not* participated in the metamorphoses of Christianity in the School of Michael. In other words the experience of the Platonists within the Roman Catholic Church in the twelfth

century and of the Aristotelians in the thirteenth century was not carried forward by them in this historical form, but they totally transformed it in the supersensible School of Michael into a new, future Christianity.

In the second Mystery Drama, *The Soul's Probation*, Rudolf Steiner explains this metamorphoses through the spiritual destinies of Benedictus and Maria in an archetypal form. Benedictus, in his medieval incarnation, was the famous founder of a Catholic order and Maria, some time later, was a fervent monk in this same order. However, neither of them, having had their necessary experiences of the sentient soul epoch within church Christianity, have anything further to do with it during their incarnation in our time. Now they want to find (Benedictus) and tread (Maria and other pupils) the new, Michaelic path to Christ out of the pure forces of the consciousness soul. This path is built on the free unfolding of the human I which looks to the Christ as its primary source, the 'World-I', and therefore it can't and won't accept an outer body (e.g. the Church) as mediator in this process.

Rudolf Steiner gives a further striking example of this powerful metamorphosis. In the lectures about the philosophy of Thomas Aquinas he asks where the *appropriate* continuation of this philosophy is to be found today. From an esoteric point of view this means the continuation in the sense of today's Michaelic leadership as well as the new relationship of Christ to mankind which came into being through his appearance in the etheric. And the reply is: 'The world evolutionary continuation of Thomas's teachings is today found in *The Philosophy of Freedom* and in the spiritual science based on it (see GA 74, 24 May 1920). Rudolf Steiner means that *The Philosophy of Freedom* is the result of Christianity which has gone through the School of Michael and which,

through anthroposophy, became the basis for the new Michaelic Christianity on earth for the twentieth century and into the future.

For this reason one can find in *The Philosophy of Freedom*, which in its strong logical setting was written more in Aristotelian style, strong Platonic elements as well—particularly where Rudolf Steiner speaks about the development of moral imagination as impulse-giving forces for free human deeds. This moral imagination lives in pictures, in imaginations, to which the Platonists especially have a strong relationship. In contrast, the Aristotelians find they are more at home on the path of intuitive thinking.[49]

These two primary characteristics of Platonists and Aristotelians are united in what Rudolf Steiner gave as the basis for the being of the New Mysteries and at the same time as foundation for the Anthroposophical Society—the Foundation Stone. It consists of three elements: its substance is love, its form is imagination and it becomes visible through the radiating aura of thought around it. And if through the free deed of man it is planted into their hearts, then it can serve as the basis for the unification of the two streams. Thus the Aristotelians will have a natural inclination towards the light of thought within the Foundation Stone because the element of thinking is particularly familiar to them. By contrast the Platonists naturally lean towards the imaginative formation of the Foundation Stone due to their inborn inclination to live within imagination. Both streams, however, can reach an inner connection as starting point for their further cooperation through the all-encompassing substance of love of the Foundation Stone.

The Foundation Stone, however, contains a fourth element. This is the spirit which appears in the light of the Foundation Stone and which continuously guarantees its everlasting connection to the spiritual world.[50] This spirit is also the spirit of freedom which permits man to live completely independently and with full consciousness in the spiritual world while not ceasing to be a citizen of the earth.

Because the Foundation Stone was not created in the earthly sphere but in the spiritual realm adjacent to the earth, it is attainable equally by those human beings incarnated in an earthly body and those presently in the spiritual world and it can be experienced from both sides of the threshold. For at the time of the Christmas Conference this meant that just as many Aristotelians who were on the earth with Rudolf Steiner at the time planted it into their hearts, so the Platonists in the spiritual world had access to it. The consequence of this is that today and in future this Foundation Stone is the *central spiritual meeting place* of Platonists *and* Aristotelians on earth and at the same time forms the basis for their unification and the source for their mutual tasks.

This illustrates that those Platonists and Aristotelians who participated in the School of Michael feel closely connected on earth to the Michaelic impulse, i.e. to the new Michaelic Christianity which is rooted in *The Philosophy of Freedom*, and in the substance of love of the Foundation Stone which unites the two streams, of which one leans more towards the thought-light (light) and the other more towards the imaginative-pictorial (warmth).

Perhaps one could use a picture that Rudolf Steiner refers to in some variations of the Golden Legend. After Adam and Eve's expulsion from Paradise the two trees, the Tree of Knowledge and the Tree of Life, united and in front of these entwined and fully metamorphosed trees, which had now in a way become *one,* stands Michael with the fiery sword. This is how an initiate can see this imagination in the spiritual world. Today it has to become a living reality on earth through the

union of the two streams out of the force of the Foundation Stone.

It is therefore implausible that Platonists and Aristotelians cannot find each other within the new Christianity of anthroposophy in order to develop what is their main task and which they brought with them from the School of Michael, but that instead they should find each other in the old Christianity, i.e. the Roman Catholic Church. The latter would only mean that those persons in reality had *not* participated in the School of Michael or that on earth they have totally forgotten what they have learnt there, and therefore are trying to catch up in one way or another with what they failed to take on during their incarnation in the Middle Ages. If, however, somebody tried to classify them as Platonists and Aristotelians all the same, they certainly would not be those of whom Rudolf Steiner spoke in his karma lectures. Because evolution, particularly if it comes as a Michaelic impulse, always moves forward, never backwards.

Even more dubious appear the attempts of those who are trying to see something 'Platonic', as defined by Rudolf Steiner, in Tomberg's Catholic writings with their obvious Jesuit orientation towards constraint which is absolutely contrary to the principal aim of Michael and his supersensible School.[51] That this can only be an illusion is clearly understood from the above.

This illusion can be illustrated with an example.[52] The later Tomberg devotes many pages to the historical and particularly to the spiritual foundation of the Pope's dogma of infallibility.[53] By contrast, Rudolf Steiner, out of his spiritual research, says that this dogma was designed by the Roman Catholic Church 'to create a barrier [. . .] against any possible influences of new spiritual truths' (GA 184, 22 September

1918). And in the same lecture Rudolf Steiner clarifies this influx of spiritual truths by connecting it with the year 1879, i.e. with the current Michael-revelation. This dogma is *opposed* to Michael and his leadership of mankind and therefore also *against* the spiritual foundation of the earthly union of Platonists and Aristotelians.

Ignoring all this, some Tombergians go as far as to put the non-culmination of the anthroposophical movement at the end of the twentieth century down to the fact that anthroposophists, whom they declare to be Aristotelians, did not integrate the teachings of the later Tomberg and his followers—who think of themselves as Platonists—into the Anthroposophical Society. According to this point of view the Aristotelians and Platonists already incarnated today could not collaborate because the latter had been excluded from the Anthroposophical Society by the former. It is the intention of this essay to show how unwarranted this idea of the Tombergians is about the Platonic stream.

In addition one will not find the slightest reference to the Michael Mystery of the present time anywhere in Tomberg's later works or any mention that Michael is the spirit of our time and that he sets mankind very special tasks. This fact is even more significant because only precise knowledge of Michael's *present* task, on which the reappearance in the etheric directly depends, can lead mankind to participate in it consciously. 'Only if the rule of Michael expands more and more can the event of the appearance of the Christ come about' (GA 158, 9 November 1914). For this reason Rudolf Steiner strove so hard, right up to the end of his life, to reveal the cosmic Michael Mystery to mankind. Tomberg, however, mentions Michael only fleetingly in his *Meditations on the Tarot* and usually within the traditional context of the Church. Not a word concerning Michael's present mission or his crucial relationship to the reappearance in the etheric can be found there.

This provides further evidence that the 'Platonists' spoken of in connection with Tomberg's later writings have no relationship to Michael and can therefore not be described as those of whom Rudolf Steiner spoke in his lectures as the Michael-pupils. Tomberg stated, 'The Michael-impulse is that of the time spirit, which means that any spiritual striving in the present time that disregards him is either retarded or erratic, in other words cannot be regarded as healthy,' which shows that he held a different view during his 'anthroposophical' period to the one he represented later.[54] And because one cannot find any indication of the Michael Mystery of the present—and hence no connection to the spirit of the time—every reader is left to judge Tomberg's later works for himself.

All this throws light on the words of Rudolf Steiner, which may at first puzzle the reader, about the association of the anthroposophical movement with 'other spiritual streams' (GA 237, 28 July 1924). This is not the place to define 'other spiritual streams' further. What can be said with absolute certainty, however, is what these streams are *not*. And that means that under no circumstances did Rudolf Steiner refer to those streams which have an anti-Michaelic character or, as in the case of Tomberg, support the dogma of infallibility in their fight against the present impulse of the consciousness soul. Michael is the spirit who always leads mankind towards the future. Therefore in those streams which fight against the basic character of our epoch and wish to preserve the past under all circumstances, Michael's impulse is ignored. 'That is the real fight that Rome leads against the world; this Rome wants to hold onto something that is useful for the intellectual soul, whilst mankind wants to proceed in its development towards the consciousness soul' (GA 185, 19 October 1918).

*

Finally I would like to point to a further aberration. Some Tombergians claim that within anthroposophy insufficient emphasis is put on the forces of the Sophia and one therefore has to look for these forces somewhere else, for example in the later Tomberg or in the veneration of Mary by the Catholic Church. The reality, however, is different. Through anthroposophy the forces of the Sophia begin to work for the first time in earthly development within the conscious and now independent human being. The name 'Anthroposophy' points to this not indirectly but very concretely. Sophia today wishes to connect with the individual human being who has come of age. Hence Rudolf Steiner can address her directly as Anthropos-*Sophia* (Anthroposophia), pointing to the fact that we are dealing with a being of the spiritual world whose task it is today to connect mankind with the divine Sophia.[55]

Those, however, who are looking for the Sophia-impulse elsewhere don't know (or have forgotten) that, after the School of Michael had taken place, all of heavenly anthroposophy was reborn as the future form of Christianity within the supersensible cultus[56] in the second stage of its cosmic preparation, i.e. in the sphere of the Imagination with which the being of Sophia is directly connected. Or one could say: Out of Michael's Sun-sphere anthroposophy went through the imaginative sphere of Sophia in order to become the source of the new Christianity on earth. Thus the heavenly Sophia is connected as deeply to anthroposophy through the supersensible cultus as is Michael through his supersensible School. Both stages of the heavenly preparation of anthroposophy carry in their centre the *new Christianity* and its central task—to prepare mankind in the epoch of freedom that Christ will walk amongst them in his etheric form from the twentieth century onwards.

Right from the beginning it was Rudolf Steiner's most important mission to bring this knowledge to mankind and thereby facilitate a conscious meeting of mankind and the etheric Christ, and he fulfilled this instruction given by Michael and Sophia for our epoch of the consciousness soul out of the forces of the School of Michael and the supersensible cultus.

On this path of anthroposophy all true Platonists and Aristotelians will follow him united.

Appendix

An Illusion and its Consequences
(First published in *Nachrichtenblatt* No. 4, 20 April 1997.)

The first reaction to the second, enlarged edition of *The Case of Valentin Tomberg, Anthroposophy or Jesuitism*[57] was an article by Michael Frensch entitled: 'Valentin Tomberg and the Bodhisattva Question' (*Novalis* 12/1, 1996/97). A dedicated follower of Tomberg answers the question as to what Tomberg's attitude was to the rumour, circulated by his admirers, that he might be the Bodhisattva of the twentieth century predicted by Rudolf Steiner.

Tomberg's opinion on this had not hitherto been documented besides reports that in the sixties some anthroposophists from Central Europe had travelled to England with this question and Tomberg is said to have replied with a decisive 'No'. As all other circumstances surrounding this discussion, as well as the names of the participants having remained anonymous, this problem could not be dealt with further.

In his article Michael Frensch has now published two authentic witness reports of close friends of Tomberg from Holland in the forties. In a letter dating from 1989 the anthroposophist Jan van der Most informs Mr Frensch of the following:

> During a discussion in Amsterdam, where there were four of us: Maria and Valentin Tomberg, John Daniskas and I, [...] Mr Daniskas noted that it is asked of a Bodhisattva to reincarnate nearly continuously and wanted to know if

> Valentin's incarnations could have something to do with this, and whether this was why so many people asked if he was the Maitreya-Bodhisattva. Valentin was really very shocked and annoyed that this was thought of him: *No, no, I am not the Maitreya!* It was as if he heard for the very first time that this was what 'people in England whispered', 'Leute in Holland fluisterden' and 'Leute in Deutschland flüsterten'; and he wanted nothing further to do with this...' [italics Frensch].

A further document is the stenograph by the anthroposophist Frau van Rijnberk of Tomberg's so-called *Esoteric News* (approx. 1942/43), which confirms that Tomberg still awaited the future appearance of the Maitreya-Bodhisattva in the forties.

With this publication by Frensch the suggestion that Tomberg might have been the Maitreya-Bodhisattva is refuted. The only question remaining is to what purpose Tomberg's followers circulated this suggestion, openly or secretly, within anthroposophical circles for decades?[58] And why were these witness statements by van der Most and van Rijnberk only published in 1996/97 although they are more than 40 years old and Mr Frensch knew about them since 1989 at the earliest?

This long overdue correction of an error reopens the problem about anthroposophy or Jesuitism in the life and work of Valentin Tomberg. In this case the problem does not lie alone in the revelation of the earthly identity of the Bodhisattva, but predominantly in the consolidation of the Bodhisattva with the Jesuit stream through Tomberg's later works. Still today the strongest defence of Jesuitism comes from the circles of Tomberg followers, as documented by the October issues of the magazine *Novalis* (1996) which carries Jesuitism as its theme under the banner: 'Jesuits—Cross without Roses?' The different articles all ascribe the Cross *with* Roses to Jesuitism in order to make it compatible with Rosicrucianism.

In this issue of *Novalis* the anthroposophical-Rosicrucian schooling path, which is described for example in *Knowledge of the Higher Worlds*, is depicted as being similar to the Ignatian exercises: 'Both paths lead to a common goal—as long as they are practised correctly and truly' (Seiss, p. 77). This is absolutely contrary to Rudolf Steiner's statement about Jesuitism: 'It is unlikely that there exists a greater discrepancy in the cultural development of the last centuries than that between Jesuitism and Rosicrucianism' (GA 131, lecture of 5 October 1911). In order to solve this contradiction the writers attempt to portray Rudolf Steiner's most important statements on this subject as 'a one-sided picture of the [Ignatian] exercises' (Salman, p. 10), as 'completely erroneous' (Mennekes, p. 35), as 'misinterpretation' (Grom, p. 73) or as 'requiring urgent correction' (Maas, p. 83). Within the whole publication there is not one voice standing up for Rudolf Steiner and anthroposophy.[59]

The background to this publication is no doubt the fact that in his later work Tomberg puts the Maitreya-Bodhisattva's pursuits under the sign of Jesuitism and offers this to the public as a conclusion to the impulse of Ignatius Loyola.[60] Therefore Tomberg's later works have to be understood as an attack on the future work of the Maitreya-Bodhisattva for humanity and hence also an attack on the etheric Christ, because this also includes an attempt to lead his reappearance into the path of the Jesuits. Our book aims to make a contribution to clarify and correct the illusions and conjectures linked to this problem.

In Place of an Epilogue

Six years after its publication *The Case of Valentin Tomberg* remains topical, particularly in view of the development of the Tombergian stream. Furthermore, every anthroposophist who really wishes to understand and judge for himself the problem of the debate between anthroposophy and Tombergianism will have to read the complete contents of the issue of *Novalis* mentioned on pp. 39–41, as the articles are the direct product of the alliance of its authors with Tomberg's later Catholic works.

In order to judge the contents of this issue one also needs to take note of the article by Armin Husemann mentioned earlier (see note 59), in which he completely refutes the argumentation by the main author of this issue in his attempt to discredit Rudolf Steiner's judgement of Jesuitism.

In addition a further attempt by some Tombergians to eliminate the unavoidable dispute between anthroposophy and Jesuitism may be noted, where it is claimed that apparently, towards the end of his life, Rudolf Steiner changed his opinion about Jesuitism as clearly depicted and justified in his first lecture of the cycle *From Jesus to Christ* (1911). As main proof for this claim stands a quote from the end of the fifth lecture of the *Apocalypse* cycle (GA 346, 9 September 1924) for priests of the Christian Community. But what Rudolf Steiner says there can only be used if one doesn't pay attention to, or omits altogether, the key phrase.[61] This phrase is 'shadow counter-image'.[62] That means: the inner path of the priests of the Christian Community, which is completely anchored in anthroposophy, relates to the path of the Ignatian exercises as light does to shadow. It is hardly possible to make the difference between the Jesuit schooling path and all that is created out of anthroposophy any more apparent.

In addition, the above-mentioned lecture by Rudolf Steiner uses the same words he used 13 years earlier in the cycle *From Jesus to Christ* to describe the Jesuits and their occult practices. In 1924 (as already in 1911) the impulse of Ignatius Loyola appears to him as 'very one-sided', even 'extremely one-sided' (GA 346). This shows the resolute consistency with which Rudolf Steiner maintained his judgement of the Jesuit schooling path right up to the end of his life.

In her critique of the book *The Case of Valentin Tomberg* in *Novalis* (issue 1/2, 2003), L. Heckmann quotes the words spoken by Rudolf Steiner to Count Polzer-Hoditz only three and a half weeks before his death in 1925:

> Always carry within your consciousness: The Jesuits have taken devotion and piety from man, they are wholly identical to Roman state power. The fight, i.e. the sin against the spirit, forms their governing supremacy, the only sin of which the scripture says that it will not be forgiven [Matt. 12:31]. And yet the spirit cannot be wiped out completely but only few will carry it into the future.

These words by Rudolf Steiner have to be taken particularly seriously in view of the arson attack on the first Goetheanum and the direct attack on his health during the last days of the Christmas Conference.[63]

That the author of the first volume of Tomberg's biography has become aware of these words is already a positive step. It would be desirable that when writing the second volume, which deals with the Catholic period in Tomberg's life, these words by Rudolf Steiner be juxtaposed with what Tomberg really wrote about Ignatius Loyola, his exercises and the Order of Jesuits in the second part of his life.[64] Only out of this comparison can one understand the inner change in Tomberg's life and being, as well as to his relationship to anthroposophy and Rudolf Steiner to which the letter cited at the beginning of this essay bears witness in a most shocking way.

Notes

1. For example: Charles Lawrie, 'V. Tomberg: Some facts, some questions', in *Shoreline*, No. 2, 1989; and M. Kriele: publisher's concluding remarks to V. Tomberg's book *Lazarus komm heraus*, Basel 1985.
2. For example in M. Kriele, *Anthroposophie und Kirche*, Herder Verlag, 1996.
3. The original letter was written in German, as follows:
Sehr geehrter Herr [. . .]
Hier folgt eine späte—aber gereifte—Antwort auf Ihren Brief vom 15.1. 1970, den ich sehr sorgfältig gelesen, durchdacht habe. Meine Hauptfrage und -sorge ist, wie ich Ihnen eine kostspielige Enttäuschung ersparen könnte. Denn eine Enttäuschung, wenn Sie nach Reading kommen, und mich persönlich kennen lernen, ist unvermeidlich, da Sie denjenigen, der als Autor der «Betrachtungen» in den dreißiger Jahren auftrat und der eine aufs Zentrale wiederorientierte Geisteswissenschaft vertrat, nicht treffen werden—und zwar aus dem einfachen Grunde, daß er nicht mehr da ist, daß er nicht mehr existiert.
Der Autor der «Betrachtungen» über die Bibel und das Evangelium war ein Mensch, der sich als Aufgabe es gestellt hatte, das Lebenswerk Rudolf Steiners—die Geisteswissenschaft—dadurch vor Verflachung und Sklerose zu retten, indem sie wiederum auf das Zentrale hin orientiert werden sollte. Nun ist der «innere Nachfolger» desselben Menschen heute der Ansicht, daß es keine «Geisteswissenschaft» gibt und geben kann. Denn eine noch so aufs Zentrale hin orientierte «Geisteswissenschaft» kann nur Wasser für die Mühle des Todes liefern. Denn sie wird unvermeidlich intellektuell schematisiert und «foscilisiert» werden. Auch gab es nie eine Geisteswissenschaft, da ja das Grundkriterium jeder Wissenschaft—die Nachprüfbarkeit und Allgemeingültigkeit—nicht vorhanden war.

Sie war in Wirklichkeit, wenn aufs Religiöse bezogen—freie Theologie oder ≪Theologie auf eigene Faust≫ wenn aufs Anthropologisch und Psychologisch bezogen, die Verallgemeinerung der persönlichen tiefenpsychologischen Erfahrungen. Während die Erfahrungen selbst Mystik sind, also keinerlei Wissenschaftlichkeit—Allgemeingültigkeit und Nachprüfbarkeit—beanspruchen können.

Folglich beruht letzten Endes die Überzeugungskraft der sog. ≪Geisteswissenschaft≫, psychologisch auf der gläubigen Zustimmung, die eine Gruppe besonders gearteter Menschen ihr entgegenbringt; objektiv, aber auf dem Vertrauen der Zeugenaussage gegenüber, das heißt Autorität. Kein Papst hat je das Maß des Vertrauens ihm persönlich der Menschheit zugemutet und beansprucht, als der ≪Geistesforscher≫ oder Eingeweihte, wie R. Steiner einer war. Denn die Päpste vertreten die Überlieferung—mit ihren hunderten von Zeugen, während der ≪Geistesforscher≫ nicht aus Überlieferung, sondern aus seinen eigenen Erfahrungen und der Deutung ihrer, schöpft. Und gewollt oder ungewollt eine Autorität beansprucht, die mit der des Papstes rivalisiert. Also—gleichsam den Gegenpapst darstellt. Das alles ist keine Geisteswissenschaft, womit ich nicht sagen will, daß es kein geistiges Wissen gibt und gab. Aber das geistige Wissen ist nicht Wissenschaft, sondern innere Gewißheit, ein Zustand also, der nicht anderen aufoktroyiert werden kann. Jedenfalls muß er auf jeden Anspruch auf Allgemeingültigkeit und allgemeine Nachprüfbarkeit verzichten. Es beruht auf innerer Erfahrung intimster Art und gilt höchstens für ein[en] intimen Weggenossen—Kreis, intime Freunde, die das Schicksal zusammengebracht hat.

Dieses ist die geistige Veränderung, die dem Valentin Tomberg von den dreißiger Jahren geschehen ist: er hat keine Beziehung mehr zur Geisteswissenschaft, die er für gegenstandslos hält.

Auch die leibliche Veränderung seit jener Zeit ist sehr groß: er ist vor etwa einer Woche siebzig geworden, hat vor kurzem eine schwere Operation durchgemacht, von der er sich kaum erholt hat. Verkehr und Unterhaltung mit Menschen fällt ihm sehr schwer. Erträglich ist ihm heute nur die Lebensform des Einsiedlers, so z.B. hat er an seinem 70. Geburtstag mit einer Gesellschaft von sieben Besuchern den Abend verbracht: die Folge war eine schmerzvolle schlaflose Nacht und einige Tage der Zerschlagenheit!

Also, sehr verehrter Herr [...], den Valentin Tomberg von den dreißiger Jahren werden Sie nicht antreffen. Die Distanz, welche heute mich von ihm trennt, ist so groß wie diejenige, die zwei Inkarnationen trennt. Eigentlich sollte ich jetzt einen anderen Namen tragen; aber aus bürgerlichen Gründen geht das nicht. Und nichts liegt mir ferner heutzutage und wäre mehr ermüdend, als die Asche der anthroposophischen Vergangenheit wieder aufgewirbelt erleben zu müssen.

Ersparen Sie sich den Schock der Enttäuschung und verschonen Sie mich von Gesprächen über ≪Studium der Betrachtungen≫, Arbeitsmethode und ähnliche Dinge, die mir nun gänzlich fern liegen. Mein Leben ist heute Gebet und Kontemplation, davon—und nur davon—und dazu lebe ich; nicht ≪Studium≫.

Verstehen Sie mich? fragt und bitter, *Ihr ergebener*
Valentin Tomberg

4. Reference is made in particular to *Anthroposophical Studies of the Old Testament* and *Anthroposophical Studies of the New Testament* by V. Tomberg (Candeur Manuscripts, Spring Valley 1985).
5. See also the article by Jacob Streit, 'Die Zahl 666 im 7. Jahrhundert', in *Mitteilungen aus der anthroposophischen Bewegung*, Nr. 101, Michaeli, 1996. Jacob Streit knew this story from Alexander Strakosch.
6. It is ironic that on her mother's side the second wife of Tomberg who, according to some, was the co-author of *Meditations on the Tarot* (Shaftesbury 1985), was called de Montfort. She descended from the same aristocratic line as the notorious exterminator of the Cathars. On her father's

side Maria Tomberg also descended from many generations of Catholic families (her father was a Polish aristocrat who served the Russian tsar). She had been baptized and raised a Catholic and some anthroposophists who knew her well (e.g. Marie Steiner and Margarita Woloschin) believed that the conversion of Tomberg and his turning away from anthroposophy was due to her influence. (See more about this in Vol. 1 of L. Heckmann's biography of Tomberg: *Valentin Tomberg, Leben—Werk—Wirkung*, 2001.)

7. German: *Lazarus komm heraus*, Herder, Basel 1985. English edition published under the title *Covenant of the Heart, Meditations of a Christian Hermeticist on the Mysteries of Tradition* (trans. Robert Powell and James Morgante), Element Books, Shaftesbury 1992.
8. *Marie Steiner: Briefe und Dokumente*, Dornach 1981, p. 322.
9. On the central role that Tomberg attributes to the Order of Jesuits and the spiritual exercises of Ignatius Loyola within Christianity, see *The Case of Valentin Tomberg*, Temple Lodge, London 1997.
10. See e.g. GA 240, 19 and 20 July 1924 and GA 237, 28 July 1924. In the lecture of 18 July 1924 Rudolf Steiner points to the fact that Michael's most important task of the present is the connection of intellect and spirituality.
11. Someone who at the end of the thirties worked in Amsterdam in a small group with Tomberg on the cycle *From Jesus to Christ* (GA 131) is still alive today. This cycle contains Rudolf Steiner's strongest condemnation of the spiritual exercises of Ignatius Loyola and of the Order of Jesuits, and at that time Tomberg fully agreed with this, not only for outer reasons but out of true, spiritual understanding.
12. Concerning the first illusion see Appendix, 'An Illusion and its Consequences'.
13. In early lectures Rudolf Steiner often used the word 'theosophical' instead of 'anthroposophical'.
14. See for example GA 97.

15. See in K. Frick, *Licht und Finsternis*, Graz 1978.
16. See Rudolf Steiner's words in *The Case of Valentin Tomberg*.
17. See K. Frick, op. cit.
18. Rudolf Steiner also ardently warns of the occult practices of the latter. See Rudolf Steiner's words in *The Case of Valentin Tomberg*.
19. With regard to this 'alteration' by Tomberg, it is important to note that from the twentieth century onwards the cross *with seven roses* symbolizes the second, spiritual Mystery of Golgotha and thus the etheric reincarnation of Christ (see GA 265, 8 February 1913).
20. The crucial confrontation between Rudolf Steiner and the occult practices of the Jesuits can be found in the first lecture of the cycle *From Jesus to Christ* (GA 131).
21. About the relationship of the Rosicrucians to the Resurrection impulse, see in detail S.O. Prokofieff, *Die Grundsteinmeditation*, Dornach 2003, Chapter 6.
22. See lecture of 27 September 1911 (GA 130).
23. See Johann Valentin Andreae, *Drei Rosenkreuzerschriften*, introduced and published by Richard van Dülmen, Stuttgart 1973, p. 16.
24. The middle German word *Bekanntnus* is used here.
25. See Johann Valentin Andreae, op. cit. pp. 37 and 40–1. The destructive critique of the Pope which corresponds to the above-mentioned Rosicrucian works can be found in Tomberg's fifth lecture of the cycle *Sieben Vortrage über die innere Entwicklung des Menschen* (English edition: *Inner Development*, New York 1983), where he, without mentioning names, compares the Pope with Hitler in the sense that both have equally fallen prey to the temptation in the desert.
26. The Jesuit's rather strong critique of Rudolf Steiner and his revelation of their occult practices in the above-mentioned lecture prove clearly that he was right on the nail. See also S. Prokofieff, *May Human Beings Hear It!* (Temple Lodge, Sussex

2004), Appendices 'Friedrich Schiller, Kaspar Hauser, Rudolf Steiner' and 'The Tragedy of 1 January 1924'.

27. See for example the books about anthroposophy by the two Jesuits mentioned in Chapter 1 of this work.
28. See lecture of 2 March 1913, published in: *Briefe*, Part I, 1881–1890 (GA 38). The word 'again' in the quote points to the pursuit by the Church of the herbalist Felix, who introduced Rudolf Steiner to the secret Rosicrucian Master.
29. See Tomberg's letter to Marie Steiner dated 3 December 1928, published in Vol. 1 of the biography of Tomberg by L. Heckmann, pp. 563ff. See also note 11.
30. For more detail see *The Case of Valentin Tomberg*, Chapter 'An example of Tomberg's Jesuit delusion'.
31. See 'Ignatius Loyola' in Jean Lacouture, *Jesuits: A Multibiography*, Counterpoint, Washington DC 1995.
32. The way in which Tomberg characterizes, in his later works, the Jesuit Order, including its occult practices and its founder, as the central stream not only of exoteric but also of esoteric Christianity, are to be found in *The Case of Valentin Tomberg*.
33. More details on the theme of Hans Urs von Balthasar and the Jesuits are to be found in my unpublished essay in German: 'Urs von Balthasar und Ignatius von Loyola. Eine Antwort an Herrn Maas' (copies available on request).
34. In his book Tomberg puts particular emphasis on the Roman Pope as being the representative of the hierarchical order and obedience and who takes care of its continuity amongst mankind.
35. Wolfgang Garvelmann wrote about this some time ago and told the author of this work about his talk with Tomberg in detail.
36. For more detail, see *The Case of Valentin Tomberg*.
37. L. Heckmann, *Valentin Tomberg, Leben—Werk—Wirkung, Band II*, Schaffhausen 2000, pp. 346–7. About Maas see Appendix 32.
38. This bizarre situation led to absolute absurdity in Russia.

Tomberg's *Meditations on the Tarot* had been translated from the English in Kiev by Robert Powell and was published under the name *Tomberg*. In Moscow, however, it had been translated from the French where the name had remained anonymous and this was carried over into the translation. Therefore today one will find the same book twice in Russian bookshops, once with and once without the author's name, next to works by Papus and Eliphas Lévi.

39. In the same lecture Rudolf Steiner quotes as an example his book *Knowledge of the Higher Worlds*, which following the Rosicrucian principle he published *in his name* and not in the name of the Master who inspired it, in this case Christian Rosenkreutz.
40. See: *The Case of Valentin Tomberg*.
41. That means directly after the first appearance of the Christ in the etheric who, according to Rudolf Steiner, was already perceptible to an initiate in 1909.
42. Rudolf Steiner to Ita Wegman.
43. See *The Future is Now, Anthroposophy at the New Millennium*, ed. S.E. Gulbekian, Temple Lodge Publishing, London 1999.
44. Rudolf Steiner says in his lecture of 12 August 1924 (GA 240) that only through the esoteric impulse of the Christmas Conference could the demons in the spiritual world be stopped who until then blocked his speaking about karma.
45. See GA 152, 2 May 1913.
46. See GA 233a, 13 January 1924.
47. Rudolf Steiner talks in his lecture of 8 August 1924 (GA 237) about Oriphiel standing in opposition to Michael in the circle of archangels.
48. For more detail, see S.O. Prokofieff, *May Human Beings Hear It! The Mystery of the Christmas Conference*, Temple Lodge 2004, Chapters 1 and 7.
49. Compare for example Plato's totally mystic-imaginative wisdom with Aristotle's thorough processes founded completely in

pure thought and nearly imageless thought forms or compare Alanus ab Insulis' christianized, imaginative representation of 'Anticlaudian' with Thomas Aquinas's strongly logical argumentation.

50. For more detail, see S.O. Prokofieff, *May Human Beings Hear It!*, Chapter 2.
51. For more detail, see *The Case of Valentin Tomberg*.
52. Further examples can be found in *May Human Beings Hear It!*, Appendix 8.
53. See his words in ibid., Appendix 8.
54. V. Tomberg, *Aufsätze*, Schönach 2000.
55. For more detail, see S.O. Prokofieff, *The Heavenly Sophia and the Being Anthroposophia*, London 1996.
56. About the School of Michael and the supersensible ritual in particular, see GA 237 and 240.
57. Sergei O. Prokofieff, *The Case of Valentin Tomberg*.
58. In 1996 M. Kriele published this thesis in his book *Anthroposophie und Kirche, Erfahrungen eines Grenzgängers*, Freiburg i. Br. 1996, and dedicated a whole chapter to it ('Zur Bodhisattva-Frage'). He repeats this thesis again in *Novalis*, issue 3/4, 2003, despite a clear statement by Tomberg on this subject.
59. The most detailed argument against Rudolf Steiner's judgement of Loyola's 'spiritual exercises' is to be found in Maas' article. His argument and thus those of other authors of this issue has been contradicted by Armin Husemann. See his article 'Cross without roses. Jesuitism as judged by Rudolf Steiner and the attempt by Maas to pull the rug from under it' (*Nachrichtenblatt*, 39/2001).
60. Tomberg's words relating to this are found in *The Case of Valentin Tomberg*, Appendix 1.
61. This was actually attempted by a Tombergian in one of his essays.
62. P. 87 (German edition). This phrase can be found in both the remaining manuscripts of the lecture—the one belonging to the

Christian Community and the other belonging to the Nachlassverwaltung.

63. See note 26.
64. See notes 9 and 58.

List of Texts by Rudolf Steiner

The following list is intended to enable the English-speaking reader to discover where the books and lectures referred to in the text may be found in English translation. The *Gesamtausgabe* (GA) reference number to the collected German edition is shown first, followed by the relevant lecture/s referred to in the text, followed by the published title of the translation and the place and date of publication.

GA 26 *Anthroposophical Leading Thoughts* (London, 1973)
28 *Autobiography* (New York 1999)
38 no translation available
74 *Redemption of Thinking* (New York 1983)
93 (23 October 1903, 11 November 1904) *The Temple Legend* (London 1997)
97 no complete translation available
99 *Rosicrucian Wisdom* (London 2000)
121 (17 June 1910) *The Mission of the Folk-Souls* (Sussex 2005)
130 (27 September 1911, 17 June 1912, 18 December 1912) *Esoteric Christianity and the Mission of Christian Rosenkreutz* (London 2000)
131 (5, 14 October 1911) *From Jesus to Christ* (Sussex 2005)
152 no complete translation available
158 (9 November 1914) no translation available
184 (22 September 1918) no translation available
185 (19 October 1918) *From Symptom to Reality in Modern History* (London 1976)
197 (30 July 1920) *Polarities in the Evolution of Mankind* (London/New York 1987)
233a (13 January 1924) *Rosicrucianism and Modern Initiation* (London 1982)

237 (28 July 1924, 8 August 1924) *Karmic Relationships, Vol. 3* (London 1977)

240 (19, 20 July 1924) *Karmic Relationships, Vol. 6* (London 1989)
(12 August 1924) *Karmic Relationships, Vol. 8* (London 1975)

260a no complete translation available (part of it appears in *The Foundation Stone/The Life, Nature and Cultivation of Anthroposophy* (London 1996)

264 (10 November 1905) *From the History and Contents of the First Section of the Esoteric School 1904–1914* (New York 1998)

265 (8 February 1913) no translation available

346 (9 September 1924) *The Book of Revelation and the Work of the Priest* (London 1988)

The Case of Valentin Tomberg Anthroposophy or Jesuitism?

Sergei O. Prokofieff

What is the mystery behind Tomberg's life, and why did he arrive at such a dramatic change in his thinking? In this forcefully argued and uncompromising book—intended for serious students of Anthroposophy—Prokofieff suggests that behind the work of Valentin Tomberg lies a clear resolve to unite 'esoteric and exoteric Christianity'. In Tomberg's terms—and those who follow his example today—this means bringing modern esoteric Christianity (Anthroposophy) under the hierarchical and dogmatic structure of the Roman Catholic Church. Furthermore, as Prokofieff demonstrates through his meticulous research, this is the goal of Jesuitism today—that nothing Christian should exist outside the Catholic Church.

Much has been written about Tomberg over the years, but often the facts have been blurred by misinformation and half-truths. Prokofieff finally brings the arguments out into the open so that you, the reader, can decide: Anthroposophy or Jesuitism?

232pp; 21.5 × 13.5 cm; paperback; £11.95; ISBN 0 904693 85 6